HOW TO START A YOUTUBE CHANNEL IN 2024

A COMPREHENSIVE BEGINNER'S GUIDE TO BUILDING YOUR BRAND, ENGAGING YOUR AUDIENCE, AND MAKING MONEY ONLINE

Copyright@2024

Brockett Goods

TABLE OF CONTENT

CHAPTER 1: PLANNING YOUR CHANNEL ...14
    THEY SHOW YOU YOUR NICHE 14
    TO DISCOVER YOUR INTERESTS AND SKILLS 14
CHAPTER 2: CREATING YOUR YOUTUBE CHANNEL 25
    CREATING GOOGLE ACCOUNT 25
CHAPTER 3: OUTLINE 44
    YOUR LIST 44
CHAPTER 4: INTRODUCTION 58
    UPLOADING YOUR VIDEO 58

INTRODUCTION

WHY START A YOUTUBE CHANNEL?

In nowadays's virtual age, YouTube has emerged as one of the maximum influential platforms for content creators. With over 2.Five billion logged in month to month customers, YouTube gives unprecedented possibilities for people to proportion their passions, build a emblem, or even generate profits. Whether you're trying to teach, entertain, or inspire, beginning a YouTube channel can open doors to a world of possibilities.

Benefits of Creating Content on YouTube:

Global Reach: Your content material can attain a international target market, allowing you to connect to humans from unique cultures and backgrounds.

Creative Freedom: YouTube offers a platform for innovative expression, giving you the freedom to explore and exhibit your particular voice and style.

Monetization Opportunities: From advert sales to sponsorship and products sales, there are more than one ways to show your passion into income.

Community Building: Engage with a committed target market and construct a community round your content material.

BENEFITS OF CREATING CONTENT ON YOUTUBE

1. Global Reach and Audience Growth

- Broad Accessibility: YouTube's substantial user base lets in you to reach hundreds of thousands of viewers global, irrespective of area.
- Diverse Audiences: Engage with a extensive variety of demographics, interests, and cultures.

2. Creative Expression and Personal Branding
- Showcase Your Passion: Use the platform to specific your creativity, proportion your interests, and broaden a completely unique style.
- Build a Brand: Establish a personal or professional emblem and create a recognizable identification that resonates with viewers.

3. Monetization Opportunities
- Ad Revenue: Join the YouTube Partner Program to earn money from commercials displayed on your motion pictures.
- Sponsorship and Collaborations: Partner with brands and other creators for sponsored content and collaborations.
- Merchandise Sales: Promote and promote your personal merchandise immediately via your channel.

4. Community Building and Engagement
- Interactive Platform: Engage immediately with your target audience through comments, stay streams, and community posts.
- Loyal Fan base: Build a committed community of visitors who percentage your pastimes and support your content material.

5. Educational and Professional Development
- Skill Building: Develop talents in video manufacturing, enhancing, and digital advertising and marketing.
- Career Opportunities: Use your channel as a portfolio to attract job possibilities, consulting gigs, or speaking engagements.

POTENTIAL OPPORTUNITIES AND CAREER PATHS ON YOUTUBE

1. Content Creator and Influencer

- Solo Creator: Build and manage your very own channel, producing content that displays your pursuits and expertise.
- Influencer: Collaborate with brands and businesses to promote services and products via subsidized content and partnerships.

2. Video Production Specialist

- Filmmaker/Director: Create wonderful motion pictures, which includes track movies, brief films, and promotional content.
- Editor: Focus on video editing, consisting of cutting, shade correction, and including computer graphics.

3. Social Media Manager

- Content Strategist: Develop and put into effect techniques for growing

YouTube channels and attractive audiences throughout structures.

- Community Manager: Manage interactions with visitors, take care of comments and remarks, and foster a fantastic network.

4. Digital Marketer

- search engine optimization Specialist: Optimize video content for search engines like google and YouTube's set of rules to growth visibility and attain.
- Ad Specialist: Create and manipulate YouTube ads and campaigns to pressure visitors and engagement.

5. Brand Ambassador

- Brand Advocate: Represent and promote brands for your videos, leveraging your private have an impact on to construct brand recognition and loyalty.

CURRENT TRENDS AND OPPORTUNITIES IN 2024

1. Rise of Short Form Content

- YouTube Shorts: With the growing reputation of quick form films, YouTube Shorts is becoming a sizeable feature. These bite sized movies offer creators a manner to fast interact visitors and gain visibility.
- Content Ideas: Trends include quick tutorials, viral challenges, and exciting snippets that seize attention fast.

2. Enhanced Personalization Through AI

Advanced Algorithms: YouTube's algorithms have become increasingly state of theart, providing more personalized content material hints. This means that creators need to optimize their movies for better algorithmic discovery.

3. Increased Focus on Community and Engagement

Community Features: YouTube's network tab and live chat functions allow creators to engage more immediately with their target market, fostering a stronger sense of community.

Viewer Interaction: Engaging with Viewers through comments, polls and live Q&As are critical to building a loyal following.

4 Expanding Financing Options

YouTube Partner Program Updates: New financial features and policy updates may impact how creators earn money. This includes changes to advertising rates, revenue share and eligibility requirements.

Alternative Revenue Streams: In addition to advertising, creators are seeking other sources of revenue such as channel subscriptions, super chats, and outside sponsorship.

5 Honesty and transparency are strength

Real content: Audiences value honesty over polished, labeled content. Filmmakers who share real experiences and real ideas tend to connect with their audiences.

Transparency: Being open about sponsorship, product placements, and content creation processes helps build trust and confidence.

CHANGES IN YOUTUBE ALGORITHMS

YouTube Algorithms Update (2024)

1 Individual and enhanced recommendations

- Long View Sessions: The algorithm prioritizes content that keeps viewers engaged longer, focuses on viewing history and user interaction and recommends videos which can hold attention.

2 Concise emphasis

- Boost for YouTube Shorts: Allows you to see more YouTube shorts as video shorts increase. The algorithm is designed to place these bite sized videos higher on the Shorts shelf and in the main feed.
- Engagement metrics: Shorts that generate high engagement rates (likes, shares, comments) are more likely to be recommended to a wider audience.

3 Advanced Editions

- Search Optimization: YouTube search algorithms are becoming more adept at understanding natural language and context, making it easier for users to use discussion questions and relevant topics with have seen things
- Video Tags and Descriptions: Video tags, descriptions, and accurate and

detailed titles play an important role in improving search ranking and visibility.

4 Focus on quality and relevance

- Content Quality Signals: The algorithm is increasingly factoring in content quality indicators like clock time, user retention, and click through rates to deliver videos that keep viewers' interest high and deliver valuable content for.
- Low Quality Content Penalties: To ensure high content standards, non engaging videos or misleading headlines may be reduced or removed from the recommendation.

CHAPTER 1: PLANNING YOUR CHANNEL

THEY SHOW YOU YOUR NICHE

TO DISCOVER YOUR INTERESTS AND SKILLS

FIND YOUR PASSION AND SKILLS

It's important to find your interests and skills to create meaningful and interesting content on YouTube.

1 Self concept .

- Choose Interests: Think about things, hobbies, or activities that you really enjoy What do you like to do in your free time? What topics do you regularly read or discuss?
- See skills: Think about the skills you have acquired over the years. What are

you particularly good at? Consider professional skills and personal talents.
- Review Previous Experience: Review your past experience, whether it relates to education, work, or your own business. What accomplishments or projects are you most proud of?

2 Search and test
- Try new things: Try different things or themes and see what matches you. This can be through writing, video production, or other forms of expression.
- Create pilot content: Create a few videos on different topics and gauge your interest and audience reaction. This can help you figure out what interests you the most and what attracts viewers.

3 Reviews and Analysis
- Market Research: Find out about popular niches and trends on YouTube. What types of stories are valid, and where do

you see gaps that you can fill with your unique approach?

- Audience Needs: Consider the problems or needs your potential audience might have. Aligning your content with these needs can help you create a niche where you can provide valuable knowledge.

4 Search comments and verification

- Gather feedback: Ask friends, family, or colleagues for input on your content ideas. They give you insight into what you are particularly good at or interested in.
- In and Community: Join online forums or communities related to your interests. Engage in conversation and see where you can offer valuable insight or advice.

5 Define your unique goals

- Choose your unique angle: Identify what sets you apart from others in your chosen niche. This could be a unique perspective, a specific skill set, or a unique way of telling stories.

- Articulate your vision: Clearly define what you want to achieve with your channel. What message or benefit do you want to convey to the audience?

Research on trending topics and audiences

Trending topics and audience research

Understanding current trends and audience preferences is essential to creating content that is relevant and engaging to viewers.

1 Use YouTube's builtin tools

YouTube Trends Dashboard: Check YouTube's Trends Dashboard to see trending topics, popular videos, and emerging topics.

YouTube Search Tips: Use the YouTube search bar to see complete recommendations and find out what users are most likely to search for.

YouTube Analytic: If you already have a channel, use YouTube Analytic to track your audience behavior, history and interests.

2 Explore social media platforms

Twitter Trends: Monitor trending Twitter topics and hashtags to see what is currently popular in different areas.

Instagram Explore: Browse through Instagram's Explore page to discover trending trends, hashtags, and content types.

Tik Tok Trends: Check out Tik Tok trends and challenges for inspiration on short form content and viral topics.

3 Research Services Articles & Blogs

News Website: Follow industry specific news websites and blogs to stay up to date with recent developments and trends related to your niche.

Business Publications: Read trade publications and professional magazines that discuss the latest trends and innovations in your industry.

4 Use trend detection tools

Google Trends: Use Google Trends search to search interest over time and discover trending topics relevant to your niche.

Buzz Sumo: Use Buzz Sumo to identify popular content and influencers in your industry, as well as trending keywords.

Trend Hunter: Explore Trend Hunter for upcoming trends, consumer trends and new ideas.

DEFINES YOUR CHANNEL'S BRAND

Defining your channel's brand involves creating a unique personality that reflects your content, values and personality that appeals to your target audience. 1 Choose your key message and values

Objectives and Mission: Define your channel's primary objectives. What message or benefit do you want to convey? This can be education, entertainment, inspiration, or a combination of these.

Core Values: Define the values that will guide your message and your relationship with your audience. This can be authentic, creative, local, or sustainable.

2 Create a special value proposition .

What sets you apart: Identify what makes your channel different compared to others. This could be a specific niche, a unique style of content, or a unique format.

Target Audience: Understand who your target audience is and what they are looking for. Your value proposition should meet their needs and interests.

3 Create a memorable channel name and tagline

Channel Name: Choose a channel name that is easy to remember, reflects your content, and is available as a domain name and social media platforms.

- Tagline: Create a short tagline that captures the essence of your channel and communicates your main message.

4 Visual design

- Channel Logo: Be a professional and recognizable logo that visually represents your brand. Make sure it's scalable and looks good in different sizes.
- Channel Banner: Create an eye catching channel banner that gives an overview of your channel's theme and includes key information such as your upload schedule or social media links.
- Thumbnail Style: Establish a consistent style for your video thumbnails, including fonts, colors and layout. Thumbnails should be visually appealing and reflect the aesthetic of your brand.

5 Craft the tone and voice of your channel

- Tone: Sets the tone of your comments. Will it be formal, casual, humorous, official, or friendly? Your voice needs to match your brand and resonate with your target audience.

- Voice: Define the voice to use in your videos, presentations and interactions. This should be consistent and match the overall feel of your channel.

6 Establish a content strategy .

- Content Topics: Decide on key topics or topics that your channel will focus on. Make sure these align with your brand's message and resonate with your audience.

- Content Format: Choose formats that best suit your content and audience, such as tutorials, vlogs, reviews, or interviews. The perfect layout helps strengthen your brand.

DESIGNING YOUR CHANNEL LOGO AND BANNER

Creating a stylish and professional logo and banner for your YouTube channel is essential to establishing your brand identity.

1 Creating your own channel logo

1.1 is. Explain your logo concept

Purpose and Message: Determine what you want your logo to communicate about your channel. It should reflect your channel's core message, values and theme.

Style and Aesthetic: Decide on a style that matches your brand's personality—be it modern, classic, sporty, or minimalist.

1.2 and. Choose colors and fonts

Color palette: Choose a color palette that represents your brand and stands out in a crowded environment. Choose colors that evoke the right emotions and are pleasing to your eyes.

Typography: Choose a font that is readable and matches the tone of your channel. Avoid overly bold or fancy fonts that may be difficult to read.

1.3 is. Design your own logo

Simplicity: Keep the design simple and recognizable. It can be difficult to scale a complex logo and details can get lost in small sizes.

Versatility: Make sure your logo looks good in a variety of sizes and designs, including as a profile picture, on merchandise, or on promotional materials.

Tools and Software: Create your logo with design tools such as Adobe Illustrator, Canva, or Logo Maker. These tools also provide templates and techniques to help you create a professional looking logo.

CHAPTER 2: CREATING YOUR YOUTUBE CHANNEL

CREATING GOOGLE ACCOUNT

STEPS TO SET UP A GOOGLE ACCOUNT

Setting up a Google account is easy and gives you access to various Google services like YouTube, G mail, Google Drive, and more.

1 Visit Google account creation page

1. Open web page: Start the web page of your choice.
2. Visit Google Account Creation: Visit [Google Account Creation page](https://accounts.google.com/signup).

2 Enter your own information

1. First and last name: Enter your first and last name in the context.

2. Select Username: Enter a unique username for your Google email address. This will be the part of your email address that precedes @gmail.com.

3. Create Password: Select a strong password. Google recommends using a mix of letters, numbers, and symbols. Reenter the password and confirm.

3 Complete the verification process

1. Verify your phone number: Google may ask you to provide a phone number for account security and recovery. Enter your phone number and click "Next".

2. Enter verification code: You will receive a verification code via SMS. Enter this code in the field provided and click "Verify".

4 Provide return information

1. Recovery Email Address (Optional): If you forget your password and would like an alternative way to access your account, enter the recovery email address. This step is

optional but recommended for added protection.

2. Enter your date of birth: Provide your date of birth to ensure you meet the age requirements for a Google account.

3. Select Your Gender: Select your gender from the options provided or select "Rather not say".

5 agree to Google's terms and conditions

1. See Table of Contents: Read Google's Terms of Service and Privacy Policy. You can find links to these documents on the build page.

2. Accept Terms: Click the check box to accept the terms and conditions. You can go down before you accept the information.

3. Complete Setup: Click on "Create Account" or "Next" button to complete the process.

6 Set up your account

1. Add Profile Information: You may be asked to add a profile picture and other personal information to personalize your account.

2. Modify privacy settings: Review and modify your privacy and security settings as needed. During the process, Google will introduce you to some basic settings.

7 To get your new account

1. Sign in: You can now sign in to your Google account with your new email address and password.

2. Search for Google Services: Connect your new account to various Google services such as Gmail, Google Drive, and YouTube.

VISITING YOUTUBE STUDIO

YouTube Studio is a place to manage your YouTube channel, content, and analytics.

1 Go to YouTube Studio .

1. Sign In: Go to [YouTube](https://www.youtube.com) and sign in with your Google Account.

2. Open YouTube Studio: Click on your profile icon in the top right corner of the screen and select "YouTube Studio" from the drop down menu.

2 Dashboard Overview

1. Home Tab: The dashboard gives you an overview of channel activity, including video updates, analytics snapshots, and quick access to recent activity

2. Analytics Summary: Look at key metrics like views, viewing time, and subscriber count.

3 Content Management .

1. Video tab: .

   Video List: Get all your uploaded videos.

Upload Videos: Click the "Create" button (camera icon) in the top right corner to upload a new video.

2. Games tab:

Manage Playlists: Create, edit and organize playlists. Playlists help categorize your videos and enhance the viewer experience.

3. Life Tab:

Manage Live Streams: Monitor and manage your live streams, including scheduling upcoming live events and monitoring the status of live streams.

4 Reviews

1. Overview:

Performance Metrics: Review detailed statistics on views, view time, client growth, and revenue (if applicable).

Traffic Sources: Determine where your viewers are coming from, such as search, external websites, or social media.

2. Sources:
- Measurement: Find out how often your videos appear in search results and recommendations.
- Click Through Rate (CTR): Check how many times viewers click on your video by viewing thumbnails.

3. Association: .
- Watch time: Measure how long viewers watch your video and discover which videos retain viewers the longest.
- Top Videos: See which videos perform best in terms of engagement and viewing time.

4. Audience:
- Demographics: Understand the age, gender and geography of your audience.
- Audience Retention: Find out how well your video holds viewers' attention throughout the video.

5 points

1. See Notes:

- Watch and respond: Watch comments on your videos and respond. You can also filter and moderate comments as needed.
- Community Engagement: Engage with your audience and encourage community engagement through thoughtful responses.

6 Accessories

1. Channel Development:

- Branding: Update your channel logo, banner and watermark.
- Basic Information: Change your channel name, description, and contact information.

2. System.

- Home: Design the homepage of your channel, including featured content and sections.

PROMOTING YOUR YOUTUBE CHANNEL

Optimizing your YouTube channel helps you establish a unique identity, connect with your audience, and improve the overall effectiveness of your channel.

1 Channel Optimization Guide

1. Sign In: Go to [YouTube](https://www.youtube.com) and sign in with your Google Account.

2. Open YouTube Studio: Click on your profile icon in the top right corner and select "YouTube Studio".

3. Customize Channel: In YouTube Studio, click "Customization" from the left menu, then select "Layout," "Branding," or "Basic info" to start customizing.

2 Channel Configuration Optimization

1. Add parts:
- Layout customized: Under the "Layout" tab you can add sections to

your channel's homepage, such as "Uploads," "Popular uploads," "Created playlists," or "Recent activities."

Drag and Drop: Use the drag and drop feature to arrange the order of the blocks as desired.

2. Transportation:
- Upload Trailer: Add a channel trailer (a short video that brings in new viewers to your channel) or show videos or playlists to new visitors and subscribers.

3. Resources:
- Add featured channels: Highlight other channels you recommend or collaborate with. This can help build relationships with other creators and provide additional value to your audience.

3 Branding your channel

1. Channel Icon:

- Upload Icon: Click on "Branding" to upload the high quality image that acts as your channel logo. It should be 800 x 800 pixels and can be found in smaller sizes.

2. Item Banner:

- Design Banner: Upload a channel banner that represents your brand and channel theme. The recommended size is 2560 x 1440 pixels with a critical safety zone of 1546 x 423 pixels.
- Add text: Consider adding text or images that provide key information such as your upload process or social media links.

4 Updating original channel information

1. Channel Name and Description:

- Edit information: Under the "Basic info" tab, update your channel name and

description to accurately reflect your content and brand.
- Keywords: Include relevant keywords in your description to help with search optimization.

2. Contact Information:
- Include Contact Information: Provide email address for business inquiries. This can help potential collaborators or manufacturing companies approach you.

3. Communication:
- Add links: Include links to your website, social media profiles, and other relevant sites. These can be displayed on your channel banner or in the "About" section.

5 Setting up channel tags

1. Add Keywords:
- Channel Tags: Add relevant keywords (tags) to help YouTube categorize your channel and improve search ability.

These tags should be relevant to your channel's content and target audience.

Managing 6 Channel sections and playlists

1. Create a playlist:
- Organize Content: Create and organize playlists that categorize your videos by subject or title. This makes it easier for viewers to find relevant information and stay engaged.

2. Add a playlist to the system:
- Featured Playlists: Add featured playlists to your channel settings to highlight specific episodes or series.

7 Engaging with your audience

1. Updated channel information:

Content Refresh: Regularly update your channel description to reflect new information, improvements, or changes in your channel's focus.

2. Communication Features:
- Use end screens and cards: Add interactive elements like end screens and cards to your videos to promote other videos, playlists, or external links.

8 Inspection and testing

1. Previously viewed changes:
- Check how it looks: Check how your customization looks on different devices, including desktops, tablets, and mobile phones.

2. Disclosure:
- Seek Feedback: Ask for feedback from friends or viewers to ensure your channel looks and content best represents your brand.
- Adding channel information, links and contact information
- Add channel information, links and contact information

It's important to update your channel description, links, and contact information to give viewers important information about your content and how to contact you.

1 Adding channel information

1. Visit YouTube:

    Go to [YouTube](https://www.youtube.com) and sign in with your Google account.

2. Going to YouTube Studio:

    Click on your profile icon in the top right and select "YouTube Studio".

3. Go to Customization:

    In YouTube Studio, click on "Customization" from the left menu.

4. Select Important information:.

    Click on the "Basic info" tab to edit your channel information.

5. Change channel information:

- Channel Description Field: Provide a clear and concise summary of your channel's content, purpose and what viewers can expect in the "Channel Description" field. It should be informative and include relevant keywords to aid search ability.

Formatting: You can use line breaks and formatting to make your description easier to read.

6. Save Changes:

Click "Publish" to save your changes.

2 Adding links

1. Provide a link on channel optimization to:
- While in the "Basic info" tab in the Customization section, scroll down to the "Links" section.

2. Note the links:
- Add Links: Click "Add" to enter a new link. Select a URL and give the link a title. For example, you can add links to your website, social media profiles, or other related websites.

- Add Multiple Links: You can add multiple links. Each link will appear as a clickable button on your channel's banner.

EDIT CHANNEL TRAILERS AND PLAYLISTS

Preparing channel trailers and playlists

1 Channel Trailer Installation

A channel trailer is a short video that introduces new viewers to your channel, and shows what they can expect from your content.

1.1 is. Create or choose your own trailer

1. Create a Trailer: If you don't have one, consider creating a trailer that highlights key aspects of your channel. Keep it short (3060 seconds) and engaging. Include a short introduction, showcase your best content, and include a call toaction (CTA) that encourages viewers to subscribe.

2. Choose Existing Content: If you have existing content that brings up your channel well, you can use it as your trailer. Make sure it captures the essence of your channel and is of interest to new audiences.

1.2 and. Upload the trailer

1. Visit YouTube:

   Go to [YouTube](https://www.youtube.com) and sign in with your Google account.

2. Going to YouTube Studio:

   Click on your profile icon in the top right and select "YouTube Studio".

3. Go to Customization:

   In YouTube Studio, click on "Customization" from the left menu.

4. Select Layout tab:.

   Click on the "Layout" tab to customize your channel's homepage.

5. Add channel trailer:

Scroll down to the "Channel trailer" section. Click "Add" to select the video you want to use as your trailer. You can select an existing video or upload a new one.

6. Save Changes:

Click "Publish" to save your changes. Your channel trailer will then be clearly displayed for new visitors.

 2 Editing playlist

Playlists help organize your content into topic groups or topic groups, making it easier for viewers to find and watch relevant videos.

CHAPTER 3: OUTLINE YOUR LIST

INCLUDES CALENDAR AND SCHEDULE

Content Calendar and Schedule

Creating and maintaining a content calendar is essential to maintaining a consistent schedule for posting and organizing your content properly.

1 Calendar of Events.

1.1 is. Define your goals and content strategy

1. Setting goals: Set your goals for creating content. Are you aiming to generate more views, attract customers, or promote a topic or product?

2. Types of Content: Decide what kind of content you will produce, such as tutorials, vlogs, reviews, or live streams.

1.2 and. Choose a format for your calendar.

1. Digital Tools: Use tools like Google Calendar, Trello, Asana, or Air table for a digital calendar that you can easily update and share.

2. Spreadsheet: Create a content calendar using Excel or Google Sheets for a customization option.

3. Templates: Consider using premade content calendar templates available online.

1.3 is. Organize your content

1. Brainstorming: Develop content ideas based on your goals, audience interests, and trending topics. Include the title, description, and highlights of the video.

2. Content scheduling: Determine how often you want to post (e.g., weekly, biweekly) and allocate specific days for each content.

3. Include deadlines: Include deadlines for creating, editing and uploading to keep you organized and up and running.

1.4 is. Create your own calendar

1. Add Content: Fill your calendar with topics, topics, and posting dates. Include any additional information such as video tags, thumbnails, or promotional activities.

2. Assign tasks: When working with a team, assign tasks and responsibilities to ensure everyone knows their role in the information process.

1.5 is. Reviews and modifications

1. Monitor Performance: Review your content calendar regularly to monitor performance and make adjustments as needed based on audience feedback and analysis.

2. Stay Flexible: Be prepared to adjust your calendar if unexpected opportunities or changes arise.

2 Managing your videos

2.1 is. Edit your content

1. Create and Edit Video: Create and edit your video according to your content plans. Make sure all content is polished and ready to print.

2.2 and. Upload the video to YouTube

1. Visit YouTube:

   Go to [YouTube](https://www.youtube.com) and sign in with your Google account.

2. Going to YouTube Studio:

- Click on your profile icon in the top right and select "YouTube Studio".

3. Post the video:

- Click on the "Create" button (camera icon) and select "Upload videos".
- Upload File: Download and drop your video file or select it from your computer.

IDEAS FOR MAKING VIDEO TITLES INTERESTING

Creating engaging video content is key to engaging and retaining viewers.

1 Tutorial and how to make a video

- Step by step instructions: Teach supervisors how to complete a specific task or task. For example, if you are in jewelry making.
- You can take a course on specialized techniques or advanced skills.
- DIY Projects: Show how to make something from scratch, such as homemade crafts or recipes.

2 Product Review and Unboxing

In depth reviews: Provide honest and detailed reviews of products related to your niche such as indepth appliances, fashion accessories, or tech gadgets.

Video Unboxing: Unbox new products or subscriptions and record your thoughts and reviews.

3 Back Cover

- Day in the Life: Share what a typical day looks like for you, whether it's at your workplace, studio, or daily routine.
- Making of Videos: Demonstrate the process, such as how you make and make a piece of jewelry.

4 Q&A with A.M.(Ask Me Anything)

- Audience Questions: Answer questions from your audience about your expertise, personal experience, or any topic of interest.
- Live Q&A: Host a live stream where viewers can ask questions in real time.

5 Challenges and Tests

- Creative Challenges: Take popular challenges or create your own related to your niche. For example, challenge

yourself to make jewelry with very few materials.
- Experiment Video: Experiment with new techniques, tools, or trends and document the results.
- Choosing the right equipment (camera, microphone, lighting).
- Choosing the right tool for YouTube videos

Having the right tools is essential to creating high quality videos that will delight your audience.

2. Web camera:
- Pros: Good for live streaming, simple setup, reasonable price.

Cons: Usually the image quality is low compared to other cameras.

3. DSLR Camera:
- Pros: High image quality, interchangeable lenses, great for different shooting situations.

- Cons: Large, expensive, needs new glasses and accessories.

4. Mirrorless Camera:
- Pros: Compact, high image quality, adjustable lenses, advanced features.
- Cons: Expensive, system requires a learning curve.

5. Action Camera:

Pros: Compact, rugged and versatile for a variety of shooting angles.

Cons: Limited zoom capability, may require additional mounts and accessories.

1.2 and. Key things to consider

1. Resolution: Aim for at least 1080p (Full HD) resolution. For higher quality, consider a 4K camera.

2. Frame Rate: Look for cameras that support 30fps or 60fps for smooth video.

3. Autofocus: Fast and accurate autofocus can improve video quality especially for sharp objects.

4. Low Light Display: Excellent lowlights display ensures clear visibility in various lighting conditions.

1.3 is. Recommended images

1. Entry equipment: Canon EOS Rebel T7, Sony Alpha a6000.

2. Inter Class: Canon EOS M50 Mark II, Sony ZVE10.

3. High quality: Sony A7S III, Canon EOS R5.

 2 microphones

2.1 is. Microphone Types .

1. Lavalier (Lapel) microphone:

   Pros: Compact, clip on design, great for interviewing and great for recording on the go.

   Cons: Limited range, some devices may require an adapter.

TIPS FOR FILMING THE BEST VIDEO

Shooting great videos takes more than just having the right equipment; The variety requires attention to detail.

1 Organize your content

1.1 is. Create a script or outline:

- Script: Write a detailed script to guide your story and make sure you cover all the points.
- Outline: For an easier approach, make an outline with bullet points about what you want to cover.

1.2 and. Password board :

Scene Planning: Sketch out or draw special scenes to help plan camera angles, shots, and transitions.

2 Set your movie environment

2.1 is. Choose the right location:

- Background: Choose a clean and uncluttered background that supports your content.

- Lighting: Use natural or artificial lighting to perfectly illuminate your subject.

2.2 and. Ambient noise control:

- Quiet Area: Record in a quiet area to reduce background noise.
- Sound suppression: Use sound suppression materials or techniques to reduce echoes and unwanted sounds.

3 Customize the camera settings

3.1 is. Use appropriate resolution and frame rate:

- Resolution: Shoot in at least 1080p (Full HD) for high definition video. Think 4K for high quality.
- Frame Rate: Use 30fps for standard video or 60fps for smooth motion.

CREATING EFFECTIVE VIDEO TITLES AND DESCRIPTIONS

Craft video titles and effective descriptions

Effective video titles and descriptions are crucial to engaging viewers and getting your video noticed on YouTube.

1 effective video titled Craft

1.1 is. Keep it clear and concise

- Clarity: Make sure your title clearly reflects the content of your video. Avoid vague or misleading titles.
- Length: Keep it under 60 characters to avoid crossing titles on search results and mobile devices.

1.2 and. Add keywords

- Keywords: Include relevant keywords that your target audience is likely to search for. Use tools like Google Trends or YouTube's search suggestions to identify popular keywords.
- Natural Flow: Combine keywords naturally in the headline without clutter.

1.3 is. Be entertaining and fun

- Curiosity: Use interesting words or phrases that arouse curiosity and encourage viewers to click. For example, "You Won't Believe This Mystery Method!" or "how to find the right fit every time".
- Value Proposition: Focus on the benefit or value viewers will get from watching your video. For example, "10 Simple Tips for Amazing Costume Design".

1.4 is. Use numbers and lists

List Formats: Titles with numbers or lists often work best because they promise an organized list and are easy to digest. For example, "5 Ways to Improve Your Medicine Skills."

1.5 is. Add branding

- Brand Name: If applicable, include your channel or brand name in the title for recognition. For example, "[Your

Channel Name]'s Ultimate Guide to Jewelry Making".

2 Effective video presentation gestures

2.1 is. Start with a strong opening .

First few lines: The first 12 lines of your description should include persuasive ideas and key points as these lines will show up in search results and rankings have been reviewed.

Hook: Start with a compelling hook or a summary of the main point of the video.

CHAPTER 4: INTRODUCTION

UPLOADING YOUR VIDEO

BEST PRACTICES FOR UPLOADING AND OPTIMIZING YOUTUBE VIDEOS

Properly uploading and optimizing your YouTube videos can dramatically increase their reach and performance.

1 Editing your video

1.1 is. File format and type

Format: Use MP4 format for better compatibility and quality.

Resolution: Upload videos at the highest resolution possible (preferably 1080p or 4K).

1.2 and. Metadata

File Name: Add appropriate keywords to the video file name before uploading (e.g., "DIY Jewelry Making Tutorial.mp4").

2 Uploading your video

2.1 is. Go to YouTube Studio.

Sign in: Go to [YouTube Studio](https://studio.youtube.com) and sign in with your Google account.

Upload: Click on the "Create" button (camera icon) and select "Upload videos".

2.2 and. Action Posting

Drag and Drop: Drag and drop your video file or click and select from your computer.

Progress Bar: Check the upload progress bar and wait until the video is fully uploaded.

3 Editing video information

3.1 is. Title:

Relevant: Make sure the title is clear, interesting, and includes relevant keywords.

Length: Keep it under 60 characters to avoid truncation in search results.

3.2 and. Description

First 12 lines: Make sure the first line is compelling and contains key information, as reflected in the research examples.

- Keywords: Use appropriate keywords naturally and include detailed summaries, CTAs, and links.
- Time Stamps: Add time stamps for longer videos to help viewers navigate to specific segments.

3.3 and. Tags

- Relevant tags: Add relevant tags related to your video content and target audience. Include transitions and matching words.
- SEO Tags: Use a broad mix of specific tags to improve search.

3.4 is. Thumbnails

- Custom Thumbnails: Create custom thumbnails that are visually appealing and relevant to the content of the video.
- Design: Use high quality images (1280x720 pixels) with contrasting text to stand out.

3.5 is. Music Playback

- Add to playlist: Add your videos to relevant playlists to organize content and improve discover ability.
- Create playlists: Create playlists around specific topics or topics to engage viewers and increase viewing time.

ADDING TAGS, DESCRIPTIONS, AND END SCREENS

Adding Tags, Descriptions, and End Screens to your YouTube Videos Effectively utilizing the right tags, descriptions, and end screens for your YouTube videos is critical to improving visibility, engagement, and view ability.

1 Adds tags

1.1 is. What are tags?

- Tags: Tags are keywords or phrases that help YouTube understand the content of your video and improve its visibility in search results and related videos.

1.2 and. How to add tags

1. YouTube Studio Access:

Go to [YouTube Studio](htttps://studio.youtube.com) and sign in with your Google account.

2. Wait for video description:

Click on the "Content" tab on the left side menu.

Click and insert the thumbnail or title of the video you want to edit.

3. Change tags:

On the video information page, scroll down to the "Tags" section.

Separate each tag with a comma and enter the relevant tags in the text box.

1.3 is. Best practices for tags

1. Use appropriate keywords:

- Include keywords that accurately describe the content of your video.

- Consider using broader and more specific tags.

2. Miscellaneous Includes:
- Use word transitions related to your keywords to cover different research questions.

3. Avoid overcrowding:

Do not use unnecessary tags or keyword stuffing. Focus on quality and relevance.

4. Tools Used:

Use keyword research tools like Google Trends, Tube Buddy, or Vid IQ to find popular and relevant tags.

2 Effective Expository Writing

2.1 is. What is the explanation?

Description: Video descriptions provide viewers with information about your video content and can include links, keywords, and call to actions (CTAs).

2.2 and. To add a description

1. YouTube Studio Access:

Go to [YouTube Studio](https://studio.youtube.com) and sign in with your Google account.

2. Wait for video description:

Click on the "Content" tab on the left side menu.

Select the video you want to edit.

3. Change description:

On the video description page, scroll down to the "Description" section.

Enter or edit the text box.

2.3 and. Best practices for presentation

1. Start with a tightrope:

Start with an interesting summary or key points that will catch the attention of the viewers.

2. Include keywords:

Combining naturally relevant keywords in the specification to improve search visibility.

3. Add a timestamp (for longer videos):

Add timestamps to help viewers navigate to specific segments or topics.

4. Include CTA:

Includes a call to action that encourages viewers to like, comment and subscribe. Example: "If you liked this video, please give it a thumbs up and subscribe for more information!"

5. Provide links:

Include links to related videos, playlists, or external resources. Example: "Check out our full playlist of jewelry tutorials here: [link]."

6. Social Media and Communications:

Add links to your social media profiles or website for further engagement and communication.

PROMOTE YOUR YOUTUBE CHANNEL

Effectively promoting your YouTube channel can help you reach a larger audience, build your brand and increase engagement.

1 Benefit of Social Media

1.1 is. Share videos on forums

- Facebook: Share video links and updates on your own profile, pages, and related groups.
- Twitter: Tweet your video links, use hashtags and tag relevant accounts to increase visibility.
- Instagram: Share video clips or teasers in your feed and stories. Use relevant hashtags and consider IGTV for longer content.
- LinkedIn: Post videos and updates about professionals or businesses to connect with your network.

1.2 and. Engage with your audience

Comments: Respond to comments and engage with viewers on social media to build relationships and encourage sharing.

Polls and Questions: Use polls and questions to engage your audience and gather information.

2 Optimize your channel and videos

2.1 is. SEO Best Practices

- Keywords: Use appropriate keywords in titles, descriptions and tags to improve search discovery.
- Thumbnails: Create eye catching custom thumbnails to attract clicks and increase engagement.

2.2 and. Consistent branding

- Visual Identity: Maintain consistent branding across channel, video and social media to increase recognition and trust.

- Channel Art: Use compelling channel art including banners and logos to create a professional look.

3 Work with other creatives

3.1 is. Collaborate with You Tubers

- Collaboration: Work with other You Tubers in your niche to reach new audiences and create mutually beneficial content.
- Guest Appearances: Participate in videos from other creators or invite them into your channel for interviews or collaborative projects.

3.2 and. Network with influencers .

- Influential Outreach: Reach out to influencers or bloggers in your niche for cross promotional opportunities or guest appearances.

4 Use paid advertising

4.1 is. YouTube Advertising

- Video Ads: Create complex video ads to promote your specific channel or video. Use True View ads to select whether viewers want to see them.
- Display ads: Use display ads to appear in YouTube search results or related video pages.

4.2 and. Social Media Advertising

Targeted Campaigns: Create targeted ad campaigns on platforms like Facebook, Instagram and Twitter to reach your ideal audience.

5 Participating in Community Building

5.1 is. Join the online community

- Forums and Groups: Join forums and online communities related to your niche. Share your knowledge and cleverly promote your channel.
- Subreddits: Participate in relevant subreddits and share your comments

where appropriate following community guidelines.

SOCIAL MEDIA STRATEGIES

Social Media Strategies To Promote Your YouTube Channel

Effective use of social media can increase the visibility and engagement of your YouTube channel.

1 Define your social media goals

1.1 is. Set goals .

Awareness: Increase brand awareness and reach a wider audience.

Engagement: Drive more interaction and build a community around your content.

Traffic: Drive traffic to your YouTube channel and videos.

1.2 and. Special Features .

Engagement Rate: Likes, Shares, Comments and Interactions.

Referral Traffic: Click through rates and traffic sent from social media to your YouTube channel.

Improvement: Increase in followers and subscribers.

2 Select the appropriate platforms

2.1 is. Stage Selection .

- Facebook: Good for building community and sharing video content in groups and pages.
- Twitter: Useful for real time updates, interacting with followers and using hashtags.
- Instagram: Great for visual content, stories, reels, and younger audience engagement.
- LinkedIn: Ideal for business content and business oriented audiences.
- TikTok: Works great for short, interesting video clips and trends.

2.2 and. Tailor content for any platform

Format: Customize the content format and style to fit best practices on each platform.

Audience: Understand the preferred audience and specific behaviors of each platform.

3 Be interesting

3.1 is. Share teasers and highlights

Video Snippets: Share short clips or trailers of your YouTube videos to entice viewers to watch the entire video.

Behind the Scenes: Post behind the scenes content or bloopers to give a personal touch and build engagement.

3.2 and. Use images and photos

Eye catching thumbnails: Use your video thumbnails or create custom graphics to grab attention.

Info graphics: Share info graphics or visual summaries of your video content.

3.3 and. Post often

Content Calendar: Create a content calendar to schedule and schedule regular posts.

Time: Post at the best times when your audience is most active.

4 Connect with your audience

4.1 is. Reply to comments and messages

Timely Response: Communicate with followers by quickly responding to their comments and messages.

Build relationships: Develop relationships and appreciate the support of the audience.

REPLY TO COMMENTS AND COMMENTS ON YOUTUBE

Connecting with your audience by responding to comments and comments is essential to building a strong community and keeping viewers loyal.

1 Post report

1.1 is. Processed comments report .

YouTube Studio: Go to [YouTube Studio](https://studio.youtube.com) and click on the "Settings" tab.

Feedback: In the "Feedback" section, make sure notifications are enabled for feedback on new connections.

1.2 and. Monitor Reporting

Email Alerts: Set up email notifications for comments to monitor communications that YouTube Studio doesn't need to monitor all the time.

2 Respond quickly and thoughtfully

2.1 is. The right time

Respond Promptly: Aim to respond to comments within 2448 hours to keep the conversation active and show that you value caregiver involvement.

2.2 and. Personalization

Address viewers by name: Use the commencement's name or signature in the reply to make the communication feel more personal.

Appropriate Response: Provide a thoughtful, specific response to the allegations or allegations.

3 Edit types of information

3.1 is. Good News

Show Appreciation: Thanks to the viewers for their positive comments and thanks for their support. Example: "Thank you for being kind you